Two·Trees

Two · Trees

poems

ELLEN BRYANT VOIGT

Ellen Bryant Voigt

*For Alison —
Warm good wishes*

W·W·NORTON & COMPANY

NEW YORK   LONDON

4-4-02

Printed in the United States of America

FIRST EDITION

The text of this book is composed in Clearface,
with the display set in Peach Update.
Composition by PennSet, Inc.
Manufacturing by the Courier Companies, Inc.
Book design by Debra Morton Hoyt.

Library of Congress Cataloging-in-Publication Data
Voigt, Ellen Bryant
    Two trees : poems / Ellen Bryant Voigt.
      p. cm.
    I. Title.
  PS3572.034T87   1992
811'.54—dc20   91-46315

ISBN 0-393-03392-9

W.W. Norton & Company, Inc., 500 Fifth Avenue, New York, N.Y. 10110
W.W. Norton & Company Ltd., 10 Coptic Street, London WC1A 1PU

1 2 3 4 5 6 7 8 9 0

for Lee Hampton Benton

CONTENTS

ACKNOWLEDGMENTS

The poems in this collection first appeared in the
following journals and anthologies:

American Poetry Review: "Variations: The Innocents"
Antioch Review: "The Letters," "Woman Who Weeps"
Atlantic: "At the Piano," "Song and Story"
Erato/Harvard Book Review: "The Innocents"
New England Review: "Thorn-Apple," "Variations: Thorn-Apple"
Ploughshares: "The Box"
Seneca Review: "Self-Portrait at LaGuardia"
Southern Review: "Effort at Speech," "Fish," "The Harness,"
    "Herzenlied," "The Pond"
Threepenny Review: "The Soothsayer"
Tikkun: "Two Trees"
Triquarterly: "First Song," "Variations: At the Piano,"
Virginia Quarterly Review: "Gobelins"

Section 1 of "Soft Cloud Passing" first appeared in *Poetry*, and
sections 2 and 3 in the *Antioch Review*. "Woman Who Weeps"
was reprinted in *The Pushcart Prize, XVI: Best of the Small Presses*.

Two·Trees

FIRST SONG

Having stolen twelve of Apollo's cows
he butchered two: an offering to the gods,
and one for himself, since he was hungry.

Great ugliness defeated, and great evil: the hero
swings the monster's head like a lantern!
But in some accounts, it's only
gentle Hermes in a mask, or sometimes
the serpents are the streamers on his staff.
His task is leading out the newly dead: Shepherd, Augur,
Patron of Thieves, who had once been
Master of Invention,
                    inventing the lyre
from cow-gut and a tortoiseshell,
with which he lulled his mother into sleep;
and the flute, a sheaf of seven reeds,
with which he passed the endless childhood hours;
and games of chance, of skill,
a game of sooth played on knucklebones—
pleasures to woo those who found him
odd, and vain, dismissive
of what came easy,
                    as it was easy
charming stiff Apollo and trading up:

for the fruits of his restless solitude
the pouch at his hip, wings at his feet,
a place at the high table—
and now he shuttled in and out of heaven,
bearing the sealed messages:
half a god.
              Like the gods, a youth
with multiple gifts and single-mindedness
can make himself invisible; and this is how
he came, in foulest weather, to the cave,
where the Fates, Triple-Goddess of the Moon,
weave and cut the stories, the human lives,
just one tooth among them,
just one eye:
              with the eye he saw
the magnitude of what he'd thrown away,
who gave the world the musical scale,
sounds become a sweetness and a power;
who gave the world the alphabet,
the mind made supple as the hand;
who gave the world hymns of invocation,
seven vowels uttered in succession,
so mortals might petition
blind fortune;
              and he cast his fortune
when he cast the tooth, and knew
whether those on earth were lost or blest,
beauty would divide them,

and each unwind as on a spindle rod
until the blade settles against the thread—
with no more than a flutter in the air
he's there at the bloody couch,
God of Contracts,
                    God of Silence,
who lays the golden staff across their eyes.

EFFORT AT SPEECH

Nothing was as we'd thought, the sea
anemones not plants but animals,
flounder languishing on the sand
like infants waiting to be turned—
from the bottom we followed the spiral ramp
around and up, circling the tank.
Robert, barely out of the crib,
rode his father's shoulders, uttering
words or parts of words and pointing
ceaselessly toward the water, toward some
one of the many shapes in the water,
what he could not name, could not describe.
Starfish, monkfish—not fish—catfish,
sea hare, sea horse: we studied the plaques
for something to prompt him with,
but he tucked his head as if shamed.
So I left them at the school of the quick
yellow-with-black-stripes conventional,
passed the armored centenary
turtle going down as I went up,
seaweed, eels, elongate gun-gray suede
bodies of the prehistoric sharks
transversing the reef, and headed to the top,
thinking to look down through the multiple layers.
When it first came at me, it seemed more
creature of the air than of the sea,
huge, delta-winged, bat-winged,
head subsumed in the spread pectorals—

unless it was all head—a kite
gliding to the wall between us, veering
up, over, exposing its light belly,
"face" made by gill-slits opening,
the tail's long whip and poison spine.
Eagle Ray: Cordata, like the eagle;
it skated along the glass—
eagle scanning the sheer canyon wall,
bat trapped inside the cave,
no, like a mind at work, at play,
I felt I was seeing through the skull—
and then away.

for William Meredith

AT THE PIANO

At the piano, the girl, as if rowing upstream,
is driving triplets against the duple meter,
one hand for repetition,
one hand for variation and for song.
She knows nothing, but Bach knows everything.
Outside, in the vast disordered world,
the calves have been taken from their mothers;
both groups bawled and hooted all night long—
she heard them from her quilted double bed.
Twice a day, she gives the young
their frothy warm placebo. While her brother
steadies the cow with grain, her sister
leans in close from the little stool,
fingertips aligned on the wrinkled tits
as if to pick some soft, fleshy fruit
but pressing in, hard, while pulling down,
she milks with both hands, two jets of milk
spraying the metal pail as they go in.
The girl must put her whole hand in the pail
and push the head of the suckling toward it:
wet muzzle, corrugated tongue:
when her last year's calf was in the bank
she drew the money out for candlesticks,
a present for her parents—tall and brass
because she thought the eighteenth was for brass.
Hers was the only gift. Her mother filled them
with thin candles, never lit—they are twin lighthouses
on the mantel, twinned again by the watery mirror

and flanking the loud squat clock, her metronome.
At the piano, hands in her lap—
what's given, and what's made from luck and will—
she also hears a diaphonic moan:
long before dusk the animals in the pens
again have started calling for each other,
either hungry or too full, she can't tell
which is which. Her mother's in the kitchen,
her father's in the hayloft pitching hay,
she pushes off in her wooden boat—
she knows nothing, she thinks
no one could be happier than this.

Variations: AT THE PIANO

The almost visible wall
is made of sound.
It keeps the girl apart
as she prefers,
as long as her fingers
press the even keys,
as long as the household
hears the web of sound
spun from the loom.

Outside, in mild
or terrible weather, trees
bud, flower, leaf out,
lose leaves. Inside,
the king and queen have swooned,
the castle swoons.

Wall of gauze, of glass.

True pitch:
when the eye can hear,
when the ear names what's heard:
the mind becomes a second instrument.

Transposing the world to one mathematic A,
she envies how the others
steer by the wake of any passing ship.
Fixed to a fixed star, she becomes the star—
that distant—
a flare in the crowded heavens.

The day is foul—a thin sleet falling everywhere,
the slops of it congealing on the street
with trash, soot, smog and general grime,
the sky's dark clouds incarnate underfoot,
buses, cars, people, rats, roaches
flooding the street with their effluvia.
Inside the studio, it's high summer,
eighteenth-century rational Germany.
On the open score a meadow blooms, the notes
flowers on their upright stems, the pianist
harvesting from each its grain of sound—
she has, that is, the undeflected focus
of a bee, and from the concert grand
the fugue emerging—

                    see how it seduces,
what carries no mark of the present world,
no news, no merchants, no murderous weather,
no crude alarms, no lives lost or saved.

"Earthy, exuberant, full of gusto,
bristling with intelligence.

And the tips of your fingers were so very small."
He leans across her arm to pour the wine.

Since thirty years have passed he can admit
he envied her her gifts—

perhaps mistakes that envy for desire,
like David on the throne hearing the harp.

And now remembers the slope of her white neck;
and now is sure that neck's improved with age.

Digging a hole to where the past is buried,
one covers the living grass on either side.

This far inland, after the hurricane,
wind on the porch sufficient
to chuff and ravel the tangled "Baby's Tears"
disturbs the cluster of chimes:
five separate oriental tones
in endless permutations—both pattern and not pattern—
as the central lozenge is stirred to strike
each of the five suspended metal rods,
the five sounds of the black piano keys.
It makes a lullaby—
                    she loves the sane
intervals of the chimes, although in a recent dream
she drove the grand piano down the road
and found no place to park it.
After a life of music the musician said,
"But music, music has nothing to do with life."

The church had no steeple, not even
the usual gable pitched like praying hands.
Inside, bare whitewashed walls,
and in the white oak benches

no color there—
they all wore white or black,
long dresses, hats and beards,
as though any artifice were vile;

likewise no instruments:
not that the boxed piano was a sin
but the wish to play it,
which set one soul apart;

but the whole congregation
knew the songs—the gifted
and the tone-deaf equally—
those slow monophonic tunes

that seemed to rise in the church
the way the church had risen
in the clearing: plank by plank
and each plank true.

SELF-PORTRAIT AT LaGUARDIA

She completes the generic oval, a feathered
drape of hair across the brow, and then I know
my own round face will not emerge. In the strict row
of linked blue chairs, she's at my left,
paper cocked to let me see her hand
as it moves, as it shaves an inch of flesh
from below the chin, sharpens the cheekbones,
the piece of chalk adept at what can please.
And soon she guesses it pleases me
when she fiddles with the eyes,
adding lines and wrinkles, returning now
to turn the corners down and darken the pupils,
installing so much sadness and defeat I can almost think
her crayon found some other mission there,
beyond intent, beyond the vanity and commerce
all around us. But then she asks,
"Are you a weird shape, or is it me?"
tilts it so I see what she means, the mouth
too far to one side, right cheek
lumped and tired.
                    And what had I seen in her
to have pictured her descending on the East Side
into the streets, the park, the train, hungry for faces?

Now she lifts it toward me, what we've made.

THE HARNESS

The lamp still lit in the studio,
the Master gone for dinner and his pipe,
and the boy in the upper branches of the tree,
taking his basket higher and higher—
Schumann repeating over and over the scales'
dull compulsory pattern—
                                    the young Romantic,
coming to music late from studying law,
lived by the old idea,
Nature Emended, Nature-as-Machine: in his mind
he saw himself triumphant at the keys, his eager guests
dazzled by the fruit he had gathered.
But what he watched by the smoky lamp
were the hands of a clerk,
strapped in the strict corrective he devised,
pulley and weights, each finger made to lift alone
and thrust, like a dancer's leg, whole days of this—

All planets in alignment is a curse;
what's needed is resistance,
the gift struck against the circumstance;
what's needed is friction, as for a fire.
After the hand seized,
he turned to the blank page
and set the ruined thing to work again.

THORN-APPLE

They're walking in early evening, still light,
his head bent toward her but tilted slightly up,
the road a paved gully in these hills, on each side
a corridor of mullein and weeds, and beyond,
the damp unfolded bolts of patchy grass,
alfalfa blooming around the crippled trees,
the trees themselves cast on the slope
with symmetry enough to let her know
they once were planted there—
                                    each detail
animates the flat abstracting mind he drifts inside,
its thick mist of dailiness and rue;
her task, endless and partial,
is willed attention: who had once been
subject and object, the artifact of desire.
Now she is the first one up the path—
the blindman's wife, brushing
a hand before her face as though
to open the beaded curtain of a door, her voice
sending back over her shoulder what she finds:
"gnarled"; then "dwarf"; then, "human,"
because the trees, seen from this distance,
seem contiguous but do not touch.

Variations: T H O R N - A P P L E

Slender, cylindrical,
without a mark or seam,
almost wet against the rock;
wearing alternating bands
of black and yellow, and itself
coiled like a bracelet.
                "Pretty, pretty,"
is what the baby said, reaching for it.

Muscular and fleet, he moves without thinking
among the shifting jerseys on the field.
In his wake the paler one,
through wave after wave of the enemy line,
presses the white ball forward: winded and earnest,
he has willed his body to this pitch
until the body is inside his mind
as the mind arranges pieces on the board—now
he cuts a wide angle and passes the ball
though he knows his friend will never give it back.
Ahead of him, always ahead of him:
this is the pattern
already set in their early victories,
one at the prow, one at the wheel.

Because it is a curse to be beautiful
and thus dismissed by other men,
the pretty man often wants to marry
mind, or grit, or great heart undistracted.
This is not the same as the lovely woman
who marries someone plain; she knows
the world's assessment has been wrong,
knows she is a fraud and proclaims it
with that mirror. The handsome man feels
no such scorn: yes, he is as gorgeous
as they say, but it's not a useful currency,
except with the plain woman who marries him
as one would pocket found-money or plant a rose.
But the plain man, the homely man, the man
hunched like a cricket or built like a jug,
who marries beauty and covets his own wife,
the man who prays at the altar of his wife,
the man who weeps when he has her, weeps when she's gone—
remember Menelaus, how he burned?

Sleek, blue, the jays are beautiful
until they speak. She used to say
that when they cry like that, a gargle

harsh as the rusted handle of a pump,
there'll soon be rain:
she could hear the liquid in their voices.

He can't remember much of what she said:
his ear is less retentive
than his eye, and when she spoke

he was busy watching her mouth
dimple and pout, her mouth
painted as he liked it.

These days he thinks of her infrequently—
when the jay calls, when the fox
shrieks in the field like a thing imperiled—

and yet with other women,
moths on a screen,
his eye will trigger something in his mind

like sound. *Siren* is the word
for what he hears, beauty's warning:
within its pleasures, all its urgencies.

Pretty face, pretty girl,
what was the camouflage that afternoon—
the way you stooped to hide your breasts?
the scabs you'd wheedled into your upper arm?
The others left to tour the reptile house;
inside the tent of net
we stood as still as trees to watch the birds.
On the woodchip path, scratching like chickens,
a toucan and a smaller cockatoo
were magnets for the eye, vivid and thus exotic.
Then I heard it: on a low-slung branch
the dove so near we could have touched it, throat
puffed like a bellows between the tiny head and fat butt—

Priam looking down from the city wall,
Echo near the pool, Charles Bovary,
Anna Karenina standing by the track,
or the one who survives, rescued from the bridge,
the poor selling fake flowers on the street,
and on the stage, the frozen prodigy
or the brilliant mind that stutters when it speaks,
the woman who sleeps with the snapshot of her dead child,
the daughter whose father cherishes his girl
like the deer whose head is mounted on the wall—

—And if the self break out of the self?
It comes to the garden wall, kneels in the shrubs,
from there maps the featureless surround.

If truth is not a thing apart from me,
then I don't want it.

TWO TREES

At first, for the man and woman,
everything was beautiful.
Which is to say there was no beauty,
since there was not its opposite, its absence.
Every tree was "pleasant to the sight,"
the cattle also, and every creeping thing.

But at the center, foreground of the painting,
God put two trees, different from the others.
One was shrubby, spreading near the ground
lithe branches, like a fountain,
studded with fruit and thorns.
When the woman saw
this tree was good for food
and a tree to be desired to make one wise,
she ate,
        and also saw
the other, even more to be desired,
tallest in the garden, its leaves
a deeper green than all the others',
its boughs, shapely and proportionate,
hung with sweet fruit that never fell,
fruit that made the birds nesting there
graceful, brightly plumed and musical,
yet when they pecked it showed no scar.

To eat from both these trees was to be a god.
So God kept them from the second fruit,

and sent them into thistles and violent weather,
wearing the skins of lesser beasts—
let them garden dust and stony ground,
let them bear a child who was beautiful,
as they had been, and also bear a child
marked and hateful as they would become,
and bring these forth from the body's
stink and sorrow while the mind cried out
for that addictive tree it had tasted,
and for that other, crown still visible
over the wall.

THE BOX

Everyday the boy marks her progress:
at the round window, her round eye,
the bluebird that scrambled in and out
with grass, or moss, with string, hair, wool,
the innermost feathers of her breast. And if
he's spotted her in the bush or on the wing,
he lifts away the front wall of her house
with the same zeal that pulls the flap
of the mailbox: it's always news:
three small wet lumps of bird, so ugly, so tender,
those automatic, stretched-elastic mouths.

What happens in his kingdom while he sleeps?
In the still yard the old dog twitches,
the swing waits like a slingshot for its stone.
But close to daybreak, like a sturdy vine, something
muscles up the slender pole—
it sways with the weight
enough to startle the grown bird to a tree
where she watches the last long inches of that body
clear the hole. Now she circles and dives, flies
to the pin oak, flies to the fence, to the pine,
flies back—speech a child won't recognize
as he crosses the grass
to where the vivid parent stitches the air,
to where, caught like a rope by the knot in its neck,
the first hard lesson fills the quiet box—
bored but not impatient,
and a little sleepy.

THE INNOCENTS

Not as one might slip into a stream,
though it is a stream,
nor as we slide from sleep or into sleep,
but as the breath of a passing animal
unmoors a spore from the lacy frond
is the soul brought out of heaven.

It is another buoyancy.
With only the briefest fitfulness
the mote hangs in the vapor above the pond,
the crumb rides at the end of the supple line
on the skin of the river
until the slick fish swallows.

    One fish, two fish, how many of God's fish
    swam out of the sea?

    Muskrat, mud rat, does the toothed water rat
    still hunt in the sea?

    Night bird, nested bird, who drew the whistling bird
    so far from the sea?

    Red fox, brown fox, can any hungry silver fox
    remember the sea?

SOFT CLOUD PASSING

1.

Ice goes out of the pond as it came in—
from the edges toward the center:

large translucent pupil of an eye.

If the dream is a wish,
what does she wish for?

Soft cloud passing between us and the sun.

2.

The plucked fields,
the bushes, spent and brittle,
the brown thatch on the forest floor
swoon beneath the gathered layers of gauze
before the earth is dragged once more into blossom.

And the woman at the window, watching the snow,
news of the child just now upon her—
she has the enviable rigor of the selfish,
light that seems so strong because withheld.
Already she cannot recall her former life.
She puts her face against the glass
as though listening.

Deer yarded up in the bog,
dogpack looking for deer.

3.

The child is hot to her hand, less on his white
forehead beneath the damp foliage of hair
than in the crevices of thigh, belly, knee, dumpling-foot.
The telephone on the desk is a lump of coal.
She fans him with a magazine, she sponges
his limbs, her hands move up and down
as if ironing: this is how she prays,
without a sound, without closing her eyes.
When daylight was first sufficient to see the snow
falling, fine as sugar, it seemed an answer,
God chilling the world to save a child,
although she knows that isn't how it works.
Her husband naps in a chair;
doctor three blocks over, drugstore on the corner—
how often she walked past, pushing the stroller.
She lifts the baby closer to her heart.
The streets are clear, the sky clear, the sun
radiant and climbing:
the shelf of her breast will have to be the snow.
And so she holds him tighter, tighter,
believes she feels him cooling in her arms.

WOMAN WHO WEEPS

Up from the valley, ten children working the fields
and three in the ground, plus four who'd slipped like fish
from a faulty seine, she wept to the priest:
    Father, I saw the Virgin on a hill,
    she was a lion, lying on her side,
    grooming her blond shoulders with her tongue.

Six months weeping as she hulled the corn,
gathered late fruit and milked the goats,
planted grain and watched the hillside blossom,
before she went to the Bishop, kissed his ring.
    Father, I saw Our Lady in a tree,
    swaddled in black, she was a raven,
    on one leg, on one bent claw
    she hunched in the tree but she was the tree,
    charred trunk in a thicket of green.

After seven years of weeping,
not as other stunned old women weep,
she baked flat bread, washed the cooking stones,
cut a staff from a sapling by the road.
The Holy Father sat in a gilded chair:
    Father, I saw Christ's Mother in a stream,
    she was a rock, the water
    parted on either side of her,
    from one stream she made two—
    two tresses loosened across her collarbone—
    until the pouring water met at her breast
    and made a single stream again—

Then from the marketplace, from the busiest stall
she stole five ripened figs
and carried her weeping back to the countryside,
with a cloth sack, with a beggar's cup,
village to village and into the smoky huts,
her soul a well, an eye, an open door.

THE SOOTHSAYER

She looked at my hand as into a bowl of soup;
then simply held and stroked it. "Strong thumb,"
she said but without praise, meaning
able to make the most of what is given.
She had a local fame for finding things—
a ring, a cow—and with such patience
untangled the year's stalled stars
that I thought, watching her kindly farmer's face,
even if she could forecast disaster
she wouldn't; that's when she raised her chin and said,
"Some people think I never tell the bad parts,
but I do," and gave me what I came for:
"Two children, but only temporarily."
Short, aproned, grandmotherly,
she tried to clarify what she had seen,
but it didn't work, and then
she said that second-sight was more like listening,
that all I had to do was want it, her voice
was crooning, voice from a dream
in which we're swept downriver,
peril of my own volition—
what should I see?
My daughter on the green rug turning blue?
My newborn with a tube taped to his skull?
Ah, heart's-blood, twin chambers of my heart,
it was long ago, before I was your mother,
she placed that wrapped package in my palm.

FISH

Fish in a bowl, cat on the rug, a vase
of wild iris brought inside.
When I start to change the water for the fish
and scrub the tank—when I dip my net and the fish,
as usual, sprint from wall to wall
like something crazed—today
when I lift one out of the water

I see my child, hands tied at her side,
writhing and tossing in her transparent cage.
The nurse was coming toward her with a hose
to cut off the air and suck the mucus out.
And since what had to be cleaned
was in her throat and she could not speak,
her mouth closed and opened without a sound
on the M, the dark ah—

like a fish, mute and thrashing,
like a beached fish. But I didn't
think that then, watching: I think it now,
this fish in my net
and me thrown back ten years.

Variations: T H E   I N N O C E N T S

How far must the fruit fall from the tree?
When the youngest turned to his new wife,
I saw my mother stiffen into grief.
Although she'd always held herself aloof
from open weeping—it was her best gift—
nothing had more branches than her grief.
We wanted the stars, the sun through an open roof,
room away from the deep tap root—the self
stirs, wakes from the safe shadow, as if
childhood had been a fever! That one brief
season, we were the fruit and not the tree.

He wants the world to see him as a horse, charging;
we see him as a horse cut in stone,
knee-deep in water.

So he withdraws. On his knees
he ferries the children, pleased to be this frightened,
across the dangerous shallows of the rug,

just as, when they were smaller,
he carried them in a pouch about his belly,
like the sea horse with its jeweled eye:

just as, long before they could be born,
he carried them in the small, thin sac.

Every seditious thought I ever thought
is in her head; and in her mouth
its best expression—
                          murderous,
murderous thoughts of those we love:
what other hell is this seductive, the self
self-justified, stopping its ears?

And where in nature is the paradigm,
except that first division of the cell?

In such a crucible,
compassion fails, but one of us
must wrap herself in its transparent robe

and speak in a low voice,
as if the other were the animal
gnawing the caught paw free.

What can help my friend in his despair?
It is his great intelligence that appalls him. That,
and the broken trellis of his choices,
if the shaped vine
can be said to choose. And now the vine
is laid along the ground, now his life, planted
in the yard, has been flung forward,
no longer held to the side of the house
but only stitched here and there to the earth
by its own frail roothairs
as it disappears among the dense grasses, his mind
not merely a blossom on it but a melon:
yes, a melon ripening, and no one
to bring the knife, the clean white plate.

On the studio door, the tacked-up typed-up mottoes:
To see clearly is to understand; and,
Art cannot redeem what it does not love.
Inside, many large unfinished paintings;
at the center, "Parents, Drifting out to Sea,"
the small boat, the foolish rations, how gulls
dove and squabbled in their wake.
Of course she knew where all such journeys end.
And yet, there came the moment—
as if she looked away,
but she didn't look away—suddenly,
each had fallen over the bent horizon,
first one speck and then the other:
the one at the helm; the one
waving from the stern her soft scarf.

The cast bread stalls, drifts in a slow circle
like a boat whose one oar has been thrust down
to the sandy bottom. The surface stills.
The little boat bobs once; bobs again;
then a long shape takes it, slams it
into the granite bulkhead of the bridge
and there are fifty fish, a hundred fish
darkening the pond—carp come out of the silt,
a cubic yard of fish crowding the slick sides
of other fish, every size of gray torpedo
trying to sink the soggy loaf that is,
by now, in ruins, defeated by
the healthy fish that climb entirely
out of the water on the others' backs,
a loose pyramid of fish, white
bellies slung at the wall, three more
minutes of this until the bread is gone.
The mass of fish likewise breaks apart.
Each drifts away, except for one large carp—
shrewd, or stubborn, or perhaps only
hungrier than the others—
cruising the spot for wreckage—

When the deaf child came to school they tied his hands.
They meant to teach him speech, the common language.
They meant to cast him down into silence
        only a little while.
They showed him their teeth, their pink gymnastic tongues.
And raised him up with exaggerated praise
        if his face made the shapes their faces made,
        if he made his mouth a funnel for the sound
                and opened his throat to let the angel out.

His hands lay on his desk as though they were sick.
Like the two sick chimps he saw at the zoo.
One ran to the wire—knuckles swept the ground—
        rolling her lips under, exposing the gums.
The other was turned away from his audience,
        fingers and opposable thumbs
                stripping the leaves from a wand of the tree.
Perhaps it would be a tool; perhaps, a weapon.

—Have you always told the truth?

I have always loved the truth.

for Stephen Dobyns

On the coast of Chile, summer to our winter,
each day in any weather the people come
with notes, petitions, mantras, lines of the verse
to scrawl on the barricade around the house
Neruda lived and died in, where his ghost
came back as an eagle, as he said he would,
crashed through the picture window with its high
spectacular view of the sea and the cliffs, thrashed
the books and papers to the floor (some say
shat on them), and sat, wings closed, like the bronze
eidolon on a Roman consul's staff,
or like the consul, with his cloak and sword.

HERZENLIED

Floodgates open upriver, the current
frothing beneath me like the dirty river
toward which he hurled himself
(as toward his drowned sister) and was hauled up,
I was crossing an iron bridge when I heard it,
his last great work, composed
mid-century a century ago,

the cello line as leisurely and sweet
as when I heard it first in the dark hall
where I sat with my life-mate, the two of us
two loons on a brackish water, for once
in concert, as they say, though one
was watching the face and one the fingers:

now, driving alone on the crooked road, I heard
the man who wrote what he could no longer play,
wrote pieces I had played when pressed, uncles
out on the stoop, aunts crammed in the frontroom
talking, *tutti, fortissimo,* outtalking
music that plumbed the new, the Grand Ideal:

and because he loved the secondary parts;
because he made the solo voice so often
yield to its companions—Heine and Goethe,
Chopin, Mendelssohn, and the young reverential Brahms,
a larva burrowing into his heart, his household—
because the will compels us and is blind,

I thought I heard,
              as the sun, angled high,
struck the dun surface like an anvil,
the rest of his life foreshadowed—
after the Rhine, a cell—
so that the Androscoggin, wreathed
in foul yellow air from the paper mills,
became, for a moment, another river, and Schumann
not merely one of the souls ferried over
but the ferryman in the prow, easing us
with a last, passionate lie.

THE POND

Eight years. This week
he would have turned off asphalt at the gate,
crossed the cattleguard, straddled the ruts in the road,
forded broomstraw toward the stand of pines, flushing a dove,
and spent his birthday at the weedy pond.
Muddy, scummed, filling with fallen branches
and grasses that will thicken into marsh—

from the highway, you wouldn't know it's there,
this postcard of the Pleistocene. At century's end
what used to be done with the hands is done with machines,
freeing another brain:
This is the progress he had labored for,
trading the mule for a horse, the horse for a tractor,
finally trading frontage off the farm.
Even in his lifetime
he could hear, from his own porch,
suburban families in their yards.

Can unexpected death be seen as willed?
He'd cultivated everything he had.
He'd seen the hillside prosper.
He believed in an actual heaven.
There are two uncompromised sites left on his land:
half-acre of polished stones we put him in,
and the hole he dug himself,
a run-off pond, shallow, subversive,
where frogs feed on the minnows, snakes on the frogs.

THE LETTERS

The drawer is full of letters. They rustle and sigh.
Sometimes, when he leaves the drawer ajar
their muffled conversation
leaks out like spices from a lifted lid.
At night he opens the drawer, stuffs in a letter—
they are not arranged
but flop and tumble like unmarried socks,
like the underwear he keeps in a neighboring drawer.
Blue ink: lined white paper: the writing on the paper
perpendicular to the lines but also prissy,
lacy as a young girl's underwear.
And some of the pages are themselves ajar, loosened, languid,
like odalisques, like figures in Matisse,
some lie on their sides with upturned signatures,
some are pleated like an unused fan.
Beside the bed, close enough to reach them in his sleep,
six months of letters squirreled home from school,
then plucked from the bag of unsatisfactory lunch,
or from the pocket of the laundered jeans,
or from the kitchen table where they'd dropped,
blossoms past ripening, from the stem.
Blue ink, lined white paper: familiar
as the letter waving in my mother's hand.

GOBELINS

We came with the children up out of the Métro
thinking about the heroes we had seen
on the large dark canvases in the Louvre, how they knew
to look directly was to be turned to stone, or lost, or to lose
whatever fluttered near the periphery,
the way we know to watch the sun's eclipse
in a blackened mirror, as one flat disk
slides behind the other:

and thinking too of the driven ones
who'd painted Perseus, Eros and Psyche,
Zeus in his various rich disguise—
who had fixed the unfolding story into a still,
not lifelike but like memory—and since the centuries
jumbled in my mind in the grand museum,
I was thinking of Monet, his paintings grown
enormous, the edges of the objects less distinct
as his eyesight failed and Giverny
fell into composite and design.

We meant to get to Rue Mouffetard
before the farmers packed up and went home,
to the plank tables heaped with cherries and beans,
globed onions and pyramids of the little yellow plums
themselves a painting—and took the old route there
up Gobelins, broad avenue
changed but not changed much in twenty years.
Freed from the map, we showed the children
the tiny bright tabac, the public baths,

the borrowed flat we lived in, new to each other,
the famous factory behind the gate, its thick brocades
in which the maidens rise from a swirl of vines—

Tapestry is dumb, my son said, like
upholstery, and the four of us concluded on the spot
we were hungry, and stopped at the next café
on Avenue des Gobelins, whose weavers
always worked from behind the frame
where knots and stitches steadied the mind,
from time to time parting the warps with their fingers
and peering through, as through tall grass, at the shape
emerging, reversed, in the burnished shield.

SONG AND STORY

The girl strapped in the bare mechanical crib
does not open her eyes, does not cry out.
The glottal tube is taped into her face;
bereft of sound, she seems so far away.
But a box on the stucco wall, wired to her chest,
televises the flutter of her heart—
news from the pit—her pulse rapid and shallow,
a rising line, except when her mother sings,
outside the bars: whenever her mother sings
the line steadies into a row of waves,
song of the sea, song of the scythe

  old woman by the well, picking up stones
  old woman by the well, picking up stones

When Orpheus, beating rhythm with a spear
against the deck of the armed ship, sang
to steady the oars, he borrowed an old measure:
broadax striking oak, oak singing back,
the churn, the pump, the shuttle sweeping the warp
like the waves against the shore they were pulling toward.
The men at the oars saw only the next man's back.
They were living a story—the story of desire,
the rising line of ships at war or trade.
If the sky's dark fabric was pierced by stars,
they didn't see them; if dolphins leapt from the water,
they didn't see them. Sweat beaded their backs
like heavy dew. But whether they came to triumph
or defeat, music ferried them out

and brought them back, taking the dead and wounded
back to the wave-licked, smooth initial shore,
song of the locust, song of the broom

    old woman in the field, binding wheat
    old woman by the fire, grinding corn

When Orpheus, braiding rushes by the stream,
devised a song for the overlords of hell
to break the hearts they didn't know they had,
he drew one from the olive grove—
the raven's hinged wings from tree to tree,
whole flocks of geese crossing the ruffled sky,
the sun's repeated arc, moon in its wake:
this wasn't the music of pain. Pain has no music,
pain is a story: it starts,
Eurydice was taken from the fields.
She did not sing—you cannot sing in hell—
but in that viscous dark she heard the song
flung like a rope into the crater of hell,
song of the sickle, song of the hive

    old woman by the cradle, stringing beads
    old woman by the cradle, stringing beads

The one who can sing sings to the one who can't,
who waits in the pit, like Procne among the slaves,
as the gods decide how all such stories end,

the story woven into the marriage gown,
or scratched with a stick in the dust around the well,
or written in blood in the box on the stucco wall—
look at the wall:
the song, rising and falling, sings in the heartbeat,
sings in the seasons, sings in the daily round—
even at night, deep in the murmuring wood—
listen—one bird, full-throated, calls to another,
little sister, frantic little sparrow under the eaves.

for Allen Grossman